Disappointment

By Meg Gaertner

level 2 little blue readers

www.littlebluehousebooks.com

Little Blue House is distributed by North Star Editions:
sales@northstareditions.com | 888-417-0195

Produced for Little Blue House by Red Line Editorial.

Photographs ©: iStockphoto, cover, 10, 18; Shutterstock Images, 4, 7, 9, 13, 15, 17, 21, 23, 24 (top left), 24 (top right), 24 (bottom left), 24 (bottom right)

Library of Congress Control Number: 2021916735

ISBN
978-1-64619-483-4 (hardcover)
978-1-64619-510-7 (paperback)
978-1-64619-562-6 (ebook pdf)
978-1-64619-537-4 (hosted ebook)

Printed in the United States of America
Mankato, MN
012022

About the Author

Meg Gaertner enjoys reading, writing, dancing, and being outside. She lives in Minnesota.

Table of Contents

Disappointment

People hope for many things.

But these things don't always happen.

Then people feel disappointed.

There are some things people can't change.

A girl hopes her friends can play, but they are too busy.

She can't make her friends be less busy.

A boy wants to play on the computer, but his parents won't let him.
He can't make his parents let him.

Feeling Better

It's okay to feel disappointed.

It helps to talk about your feelings.

Share your feelings with parents
or friends.

You can cry if you need to.

Exercising can also help.

These are ways of letting out your feelings.

exercising

Then, try to accept

what happened.

You can't change it.

But you can choose how to

move forward.

Move on to the next fun thing.

Find something you are thankful for.

These are ways to move past disappointment.

Moving Forward

People can change some things.

A boy takes a test and gets a
bad grade.

He can study harder next time.

He can ask a teacher or parent
for help.

A girl tries out for the soccer team, but she doesn't make the team.

She can practice more for the next tryout.

She can also try a new sport.

soccer

21

Things didn't work out this time.

But next time, things might

go differently.

So, do your best and keep trying!

Glossary

computer

exercising

crying

team

Index